This collection of poems flourishes like a blessed garden within the walls of a fortress. It is a miracle of life, with lush details of figs and rice and tea, of danger, longing, and love. Under the ancient cadences, under the vibrant imagery lies a contemporary tension that flashes to the surface, bringing a strong, Middle Eastern light to shine upon the rubble wrought by today's conflicts. Most of the poets in this collection are still living, still creating, still bearing witness to the struggles of their brothers and sisters. The unfamiliar geography of this poetry brings a sweet, exotic taste to the American palate. Yet if Americans can read these words not only with their minds, but with their hearts, they will come to understand that in "the space between our footsteps" resides eloquent, universal truths.

Karen Hesse

the flag of childhood

poems from the middle east

selected by naomi shihab nye

Aladdin Paperbacks

New York   London   Toronto   Sydney   Singapore

More than five hundred "calls for entries" were mailed, faxed, and E-mailed to poets, artists, cultural institutions, universities, and galleries in the Middle East. We are grateful to the many individuals and institutions who responded.

The editors would also like to express sincere and lasting thanks to Salwa Mikdadi Nashashibi of the Cultural and Visual Arts Resource. Ms. Nashashibi was, from her desk in Jordan, an invaluable and expert sleuth. This book would not have been possible without her.

First Aladdin Paperbacks edition February 2002

ALADDIN PAPERBACKS
An imprint of Simon & Schuster
Children's Publishing Division
1230 Avenue of the Americas
New York, NY 10020

Also available as a Simon & Schuster Books for Young Readers
unabridged hardcover edition under the title
The Space Between our Footsteps: Poems and Paintings from the Middle East.
Designed by Debra Sfetsios
The text of this book was set in Goudy.

Printed in the United States of America
4 6 8 10 9 7 5

The Library of Congress has cataloged the original hardcover edition as follows:
The space between our footsteps : poems and paintings from the
Middle East / selected by Naomi Shihab Nye.
p. cm.
Selected poetry from Arabic, Hebrew, Persian, and Turkish.
Summary: A collection of poetry and full-color artwork from Middle Eastern countries.
ISBN 0-689-81233-7 (h.c.)
1. Young adult poetry—Translations into English. [1. Poetry—Collections.] I. Nye, Naomi
Shihab.
PN6109.97.S63 1998
808.81'00835—dc21
97-18622 CIP AC
ISBN 0-689-85172-3 (pbk.)

in the spirit of the children

at the Cairo library who said, during the

worst sandstorm of the twentieth century,

"just keep reading!"

Introduction

Everything has changed. People keep saying this since the tragic attack on the World Trade Center and the Pentagon in September 2001.

I would like to think some things will never change:

* Our need to know one another and to care about other people's lives—if all people in the world did this, could anyone commit crimes? Certainly not.

Obviously we can't control all people in the world. But we can continue to remind ourselves of what is important and try to live in ways nourishing for human beings. It is most important to know about lives that seem, on the surface, unlike our own. We must remind ourselves and our children that the Middle East is a complicated center of dramatic cultural and religious history and the vast majority of people living there would love to be our friends.

* Our ability to grow in our perceptions, to know more than we used to know, to empathize with distant situations and sorrows and joys.

* The power of words to convey truths, across miles and waters and time.

How can we learn to live together with

greater understanding? We must remind ourselves that fanaticism of any kind is dangerous. We must work every way we can toward wider expression and dialogue. We must keep reading poetry with renewed vigor, for courage and hope. Poetry, the most intimate form of expression, gives us a deeper sense of reality than headlines and news stories ever could.

We must remind ourselves to search every way we can for the wisdom that is peaceful. And we must remember that the one flag we all share is the beautiful flag of childhood that flies with hope in every country. This is the flag we should work to serve no matter who we are or where we live.

Salaam...

Naomi Shihab Nye
San Antonio, Texas, 2001

from Letters to Childhood

Forgive me, my child,
if the name I gave you
is not the name
you would have chosen . . .

All the children of the world,
in all my abodes
you are the roses in my courtyard,
the green and the fresh,
the sun and the stars,
you are the beautiful hands,
the ones who raise the flag of childhood high.

I give my life to you.
To you I write my poems.

Mohammed Shehadeh
Translated by Aziz Shihab

"A Galaxy of Seeds"

Beginning Speech

That child I was
came to me once
an unfamiliar face

He said nothing—we walked
each glancing in silence at the other
One step
an alien river
    flowing.

Our common origins
    brought us together
and we separated
a forest written by the earth
and told by the seasons

Child that I once was, advance,
What now brings us together?
And what have we to say to each other?

Adonis
Translated by Lena Jayyusi
and John Heath-Stubbs

from Unveiled

I have always known my place. "When I
grow up, I want to become the wife of the
president," I said. I also wanted to write books,
drive a jeep, and have a dog as a best friend.

That I kept to myself.

○

"Cover her face," my grandmother told my
parents on our way to the beach. "She is
already too dark."

"Where did you get such black hair?" she
said, with obvious concern.

"From you, grandmother."

○

"It must have confused you to get such
attention just because of your sex," I told my
brother, my mother's son.

"You must have cried laughing at such
stupidity that you were better simply because
you were a boy."

"I believed it," my brother said.
I have always wanted to topple my brother
from his throne. I read, I intellectualized, I
socialized, I schemed, I yelled, I cried, and in
the end, I couldn't even compare.

○

My brother was baptized in Jerusalem. A
special boy, a special place. I was also baptized,
with my sister, by "Father Potatoes," so-called
because he was really fat. Or at least, that is all
my mother remembers from that joyous, local,
and double event.

○

There was money to be made at our dining
room table. My mother put sterilized coins in
her delicious *kibbe** dish. The trick was to pick
the *kibbe* with the hidden coin. I never won.
My brother won every time.

Later I realized the game was fixed. When
confronted by a grown-up me, my mother
didn't see what the fuss was about. "Your
brother was a sickly boy who needed
nourishment."

○

My brother was an overweight bully.

○

"But we love you," my parents said. "We
love you very much." I know, but they loved
me as a girl.

○

The boy within me was stuck with me. Not
till much later did I find out that the boy
within was really a girl.

Gladys Alam Saroyan

*_kibbe_—popular casserole made of cracked wheat and meat

My Mother's Wedding Parade

Still a child, innocent, naïve, seventeen.
A good student pulled out of school to wed.
It was arranged, it was final, it was done.
The gown was rented, the whole town paraded.
The brief private talk with the aunt and
the stepmother took place—
very little was learned. Salimeh* was not relaxed.
She shook, she perspired, she cried,
she was a child.
The whole town brought sweets in their Sunday best.
She wept upon leaving her father's modern home
for a humble two-room stone house
to share with her in-laws and a man
she knew only by sight.

She went along, went along,
singing to herself a song of prayers.
The whole town looked on, gossiped,
and the wedding picture showed a different dress
from the original one—
a wrinkled dress.
My mother was so tall, so beautiful, so strong,
her dress was so long.

                                    Lorene Zarou-Zouzounis

*Salimeh—a girl's name

My Brother

His hair was light-colored
He went to bed early
And woke up early
One day he quietly went away
Just like he arrived—quietly
　　　He was my brother

Mohammed Afif Hussaini
Translated by Aziz Shihab

Rice Paradise

My grandmother wouldn't let us leave rice on our plates.
Instead of telling us about hunger in India
and children with swollen bellies
who would have opened their mouths wide
for each grain,
she would drag all the leftovers to the centers of our plates
with a screeching fork and, nearly in tears,
tell how the uneaten rice would rise to the heavens
to complain to God.
Now she's dead and I imagine the joy of the encounter
between her false teeth and the angels with flaming swords
at the gates of rice paradise.
They spread, beneath her feet, a carpet of red rice
and the yellow rice sun beats down on the lovely garden
of little white grains.
My grandmother spreads olive oil on their skins
and slips them one by one into the cosmic pots
of God's kitchen. Grandma, I feel like telling her,
rice is a seashell that shrunk, and like it
you rose from the sea.
The water of my life.

                                        Ronny Someck
                            Translated by Vivian Eden

History Class

In Mrs. Diaz's class
we would underline the text
while she read from the book
about the great kings that ruled India.

I spent the class
doodling in the margins,
coloring in the temples and mosques,
drawing mustaches and spectacles on the faces of dead
    kings.

In Mrs. Shenoy's geography class
we learned that a triangular chunk of land
broke off from Gondwananland,
floated up north
and collided with Asia.
The Himalayas crumpled upwards with the impact.

Years later
visiting a crumbling mosque outside Delhi,
doodles and drawings
floated up
from the underside of memory.

Reza Shirazi

Optimistic Man

as a child he never plucked the wings off flies
he didn't tie tin cans to cats' tails
or lock beetles in matchboxes
or stomp anthills
he grew up
and all those things were done to him
I was at his bedside when he died
he said read me a poem
about the sun and the sea
about nuclear reactors and satellites
about the greatness of humanity

Nazim Hikmet
Translated by Randy Blasing
and Mutlu Konuk

Mr. Ahmet's Shoes

He'd spare his shoes and wouldn't walk in them
Every evening he'd clean them for the next day

He'd knock at their bottoms and listen to the sound
He'd say this is pure French leather

His shoes had a special brush and cloth
He'd always keep them clean inside and out

Every evening as soon as he got home he'd put on his
  slippers
His only concern in life was his shoes

He'd set out with a *bismillah** and walk on asphalt roads
He knew that this shoe nation would rot in snow waters

The shoes had their place reserved next to the door
Poor Mr. Ahmet would put them side by side

He'd say, "These shoes will last for so many more years."
He'd say so but unfortunately his life did not last that long

They did not throw his shoes away
Nor did they sell them to anyone as the shoes had great
  memories.

Kemalettin Tuǧcu
Translated by Yusuf Eradam

*bismillah—"in the name of Allah" (God)

I Remember My Father's Hands

because they were large, and square,
fingers chunky, black hair like wire

because they fingered worry beads over and over
(that muted clicking, that constant motion, that
   secular prayer)

because they ripped bread with quiet purpose,
dipped fresh green oil like a birthright

because after his mother's funeral they raised a tea cup,
set it down untouched, uncontrollably trembling

because when they trimmed hedges, pruned roses,
their tenderness caught my breath with jealousy

because once when I was a child they cupped my face,
dry and warm, flesh full and calloused, for a long moment

because over his wife's still form they faltered
great mute helpless beasts

because when his own lungs filled and sank they
   reached out
for the first time pleading

because when I look at my hands
his own speak back

Lisa Suhair Majaj

Childhood. 1948

Do you remember our childhood?
There was the brook, there was the palm tree;
It was bountiful and the dates delicious,
Soft and you by my side.
Early mornings were red—the morning star was bright
And gone now.
Here is white milk for you, though, warm and foamy,
Drink it, dear, take the little kids and the big goatie goats
To the riverside to graze, while we bathe a while.
No! How can I forget all this? No!
You were a child and I was a child. You dripped honey
And I collected dates.
The palm was lovely on the mound in the sand.
It loved our love, and there under the tender care of
    its shade,
It grew.
Little lovely tree, it stood there—still, dignified, unafraid
Little palm.

Alas, alas, it has all been drowned.
We saw it going down, going down
While we were going away.
Oh God, forgive those who drowned it!
God forgive us, those who have forsaken it.

                                        Hamza El Din

Growing

after Pablo Neruda's "Walking Around"

It so happens I am happy to be a daughter
and it happens that I dance into dinner parties and
   Arabic concerts
dressed up, polished, like a pearl in
the tender hands of a diver
sliding on my path in a garden of olive trees and jasmine.

The scent of my mother sends me to a green orchard.
My only wish is to grow like seeds or trees,
my only wish is to see no more death, no poverty,
no more maimed, no drunks, no drugs.

It so happens that I am delighted
by my father's victories and his pride
and his brown eyes and his bald head.
It so happens he is happy to be my father.

And I'd feel lucky
if I attended my parents' 50th wedding anniversary
or conceived a child with dark curly hair.
It would be wonderful to free my country with honest talk
planting orange trees until I died of happiness.

I want to go on following the moon—
bright, silvery, secure with the light
casting jasmine into the bloody streets of Jerusalem,
blossoming every day.

I don't want to fall in a grave,
restless underneath the weight, a martyr for nothing,
dried-up, battling against the lies.

That's why my mother, when she greets me
with her outstretched arms gives me the moon,
and she runs through the arching streets of Gaza,
and stops to stare at the white minarets of the mosques,
planting seeds of green fruit.

And my father leads me to the Golden Dome of the Rock
into debates about survival
into gatherings where friends speak of the good past,
into houses that remind me of home
into a sunny shelter cradled like a baby nursing
from a beloved breast.

There are starving children, and homeless people
hovering in the polluted air that I hate.
There are malignant cysts
that should disappear from bodies and skin.
There are soldiers all over, and machine-guns, and tear gas.

I climb slowly with my moon, my roots, my dome,
remembering my parents,
I hike up, through the sloping hills and green orchards,
and gardens of olive trees smelling of jasmine
in which little white petals are growing.

Deema Shehabi Khorsheed

"The World Is a Glass You Drink From"

As I traveled from the city
toward the country
old age fell off my shoulders.

Salah Fa'iq
Translated by Patricia Alanah Byrne
and Salma Khadra Jayyusi

Red pomegranate, juicy
swollen with seeds and memories
falls with the moon
into the hands of naked children

Tahar Ben Jelloun
Translated by Nadia Benabid

Letters

When the earth was still covered with water,
someone drew his name there, as a child would,
in block letters. Long afterward, when the earth
dried off, the letters were inscribed as if in rock,
as if from the age of an ancient king. Later,
there came the ones who overpowered the earth
with their shoes, and after them dogs with their claws,
and the wild grasses. And then the falling leaves served
as a mantle, tenderly cast down over the faces
of the dead while the good earth caused the bones
of the dead ones to feel at ease. And a long,
a fruitful sleep fell upon them. He who looks now
will see only the bare rudiments of a name,
he will remember that something heroic happened here.
And these will be sufficient for him because he
is only a traveler or because these are signs enough
for the wandering poet.

Moshe Dor
Translated by Myra Sklarew

Jisr el-Qadi*

In a place of wind and clay pitchers,
in a place of a bridge and a road,
in a place as fresh as water,
in a place where a foot touches
softly as a blossom on a stream,
in a place where a bird's passing
is only a pressure by your cheek,
in a place which means nothing,
in a place which stays precise as childhood,
in a place transformed by absent moons,
in a place of two hands, a potter's wheel and some clay,
in a place where you can be still,
in a place where the world is a glass you drink from.

Nadia Tuéni
Translated by Samuel Hazo

*Jisr el-Qadi—a town in Lebanon

The Train of the Stars

The night is a train that passes,
Up on my house I watch it
Its eyes smile to me.

The night is a train that passes,
Carrying moons and stars
Clouds, flowers,
Seas and rivers that run.
The night is a train that passes.

The night is a train that passes,
I wish, oh, how I wish!
I could take it one day:
It would take me away,
To see where it's going.
Oh, where's that train going?

Abdul-Raheem Saleh al-Raheem
Translated by Adil Saleh Abid

Class Pictures

In the last week of school
There's a camera in class, and smiles
(the teacher's in the center, wearing flowers.)
Gideon is next to Yael,
They're a couple.
Ruth's eyes are closed, she's dreaming.
And I'm not in the picture.
I had the measles.

On the last day of school
There's a camera in the yard, and smiles.
(the teacher's next to me, wearing flowers.)
And Gideon and Yael
Are no longer a couple.
Yael closes her eyes, she's dreaming.
Ruth isn't in the picture.
She had the measles.

In the class picture,
In the yard, or in the building,
Someone is always missing.

Shlomit Cohen-Assif
Translated by Nelly Segal

Sea

I'm not jealous of the pond
that's sleeping so quietly
in the middle of the forest.
I'm the sea,
I'm not afraid of the storm.
The sea's dream is always
turbulence.
If I don't have waves and storms,
I won't be the sea anymore.
I'll be the pond—
and stinking.

Shafee'e Kadkani
Translated by Ali Maza-heri

A Voiced Lament

Who's sprinkled salt in our children's milk
Who's muddied our waters
Hey, who goes there?

Are we living a fairy-tale, which century is this
Whence can the poison have seeped
Into our apple, onto our comb?

The light of day comes to our room unbidden
Wakes us and takes us away, forces
A pick-axe, a pen into our hands
The wagonloads go past, go past
Pushed into harness, we climb the slope

We pluck night from the forty thieves
Sing it a lullaby in our arms
Should not its arms enfold our sleep
Who is rocking whom?

They are walking the dead away
Mindful of proper ceremony
Is that the wind, is someone blowing
The living are in their lockers
Then who is it whose breath
Ruffles these well-kept files
Hey, who goes there?

Gülten Akin
Translated by Nermin Menemencioğlu

The Path of Affection

Along the amazing road drawn from the throat of
    recent dates . . .
Along the amazing road drawn from my old Jerusalem,
And despite the hybrid signs, shops, and cemeteries,
My fragmented self drew together to meet the kin of
    New Haifa. . . .
The earth remained unchanged as of old,
With all its mortgaged trees dotting the hills,
And all the green clouds and the plants
Fertilized with fresh fertilizers,
And efficient sprinklers. . . .
In the earth there was an apology for my father's wounds,
And all along the bridges was my Arab countenance,
In the tall poplars,
In the trains and windows,
In the smoke rings.
Everything is Arab despite the change of tongue,
Despite the trucks, the cars, and the car lights. . . .
All the poplars and my ancestor's solemn orchards
Were, I swear, smiling at me with Arab affection.
Despite all that had been eliminated and
    coordinated and the "modern" sounds . . .
Despite the seas of light and technology. . . .

O my grandparents, the rich soil was bright with
    Arab reserve,
And it sang out, believe me, with affection.

Layla 'Allush
Translated by Abdelwahab M. Elmessiri

Awakening

Darkness slowly lifts
the yawning street
shakes off the remnants of long sleep

garbage still heaped at the corners
the shops still closed
and little trees search for their reflections
in the shining window panes.

Now the houses begin to show some movement
a window opens here
a balcony there as a lovely shadow
emerges with the morning light
A little while, then quickly
the earth goes crazy
a bus appears,
then another,
then another,
and people rush forth in every street and alley.

Sami Mahdi
Translated by May Jayyusi

Poverty Line

As if you could stretch a line and say: below it, poverty.
Here's the bread blackened with cheap makeup
and the olives in a small plate on the tablecloth.

In the air, doves flew a soaring salute
to the kerosene vendor's ringing bell on his cart
and the sound of rubber boots landed on the muddy ground.

I was a kid, in a house they called a shanty,
in a neighborhood called a transit camp.
The only line I saw was the horizon and under it everything
looked poor.

                              Ronny Someck
                    Translated by Ammiel Alcalay

A Saddle & the World

In Palestine, an old disheveled street,
a wall of tiny shops, where grass grows between crumpled
    stone,
I stand and watch in the shadow of the wall.
Pots and tin pans and brooms and woven straw mats,
even handmade saddles, spill into the narrow street.
Heavy saddles, covered with burlap, to fit horses,
mules, donkeys, sewn by someone who knows saddles.
A woman in a *thobe*—a long black dress,
hand-embroidered with red cross-stitching on chest and
    sides—
pokes around the saddles.
Bending down, she touches, pats, caresses,
like a woman buying cloth.
Finally she lifts her head, then do-si-dos
toward the bald man who owns the shop
and asks the price of the saddle she likes best.
But the price isn't set in stone and will change, like the
    weather,
if you have some smarts at this haggling game.
Like fencing, you dance with agile steps around each
    other,
touch with the point of your foil, but never wound.
He says, she says. Words fly, as conductor-hands
sweep the air for emphasis. The woman nods,

and a corner of her mouth lifts. She fingers the coins
inside the slit in her belt.
"Sold! To the woman in embroidered dress!" the
    auctioneer would call out
if she lived in Texas. Or Oklahoma. Or even New York.
But in Palestine where she lives, a thousand women in
    embroidered dresses
would stand to claim the prize.
I, in the uniform of my faded American jeans,
ask the woman a foolish question,
"How will you take this saddle home?"
The woman's face cracks open, a smile spills out.
Squatting, she picks up the saddle, an Olympian
    heavyweight champion,
she hoists the saddle in the air, then lowers it onto her
    head.
She stands tall, this Palestinian Yoga-woman, her head
    not merely holding a saddle,
But the world.

                                        May Mansoor Munn

Bethlehem

Secrets live in the space between our footsteps.
The words of my grandfather echoed in my dreams,
as the years kept his beads and town.
I saw Bethlehem, all in dust, an empty town
with a torn piece of newspaper lost in its narrow streets.
Where could everyone be? Graffitis and stones answered.
And where was the real Bethlehem—the one
my grandfather came from?
Handkerchiefs dried the pain from my hands.
Olive trees and tears continued to remember.
I walked the town until I reached an old Arab man
dressed in a white robe.
I stopped him and asked, "Aren't you the man I saw in
my grandfather's stories!"
He looked at me and left. I followed him—asked him
why he left? He continued walking.
I stopped, turned around and realized he had left me
the secrets in the space between his footsteps.

                                        Nathalie Handal

Table

A man filled with the gladness of living
Put his keys on the table,
Put flowers in a copper bowl there.
He put his eggs and milk on the table.
He put there the light that came in through the window,
Sound of a bicycle, sound of a spinning wheel.
The softness of bread and weather he put there.
On the table the man put
Things that happened in his mind.
What he wanted to do in life.
He put that there.
Those he loved, those he didn't love,
The man put them on the table too.
Three times three make nine:
The man put nine on the table.
He was next to the window next to the sky;
He reached out and placed on the table endlessness.
So many days he had wanted to drink a beer!
He put on the table the pouring of that beer.
He placed there his sleep and his wakefulness;
His hunger and his fullness he placed there.

Now that's what I call a table!
It didn't complain at all about the load.
It wobbled once or twice, then stood firm.
The man kept piling things on.

Edip Cansever
Translated by Richard Tillinghast

The Strange Tale

We laughed at the past.
Tomorrow the future will be laughing
at us.
This is the world, a tale spun
by some great magician.
The living perform the marvelous play
as if they were already dead.
The stage is sad
with its curtain of mist.
And beyond the curtain,
the audience of the future watches us, laughing.
They don't see how the script
is falling into their own hands.

Abu-L-Qasim al-Shabbi
Translated by Lena Jayyusi
and Naomi Shihab Nye

Attention

Those who come by me passing
I will remember them
and those who come heavy and overbearing
I will forget

That's why
when the air erupts between mountains
we always describe the wind
and forget the rocks

Saadi Youssef
Translated by Khaled Mattawa

"Pick a Sky and Name It"

Pink

The night has come,
Pink's job is done.
She was the dawn, and the pink sun.
But now blue's time has come.
He'll be the moon,
He'll be the sky.
Pink sits and waits for sunrise,
Then she'll be the sun again,
She'll be the sky.
But sunrise won't last long.
When yellow comes
And spreads her color to the sun.
Pink sits and waits.
Pink sits and waits.

Zeynep Beler

Why Are We in Exile
the Refugees Ask

Why do we die
In silence
And I had a house
And I had . . .
And here you are
Without a heart, without a voice
Wailing, and here you are
Why are we in exile?
We die
We die in silence
Why are we not crying?
On fire,
On thorns
We walked
And my people walked
Why are we Lord
Without a country, without love
We die
We die in terror
Why are we in exile
Why are we Lord?

Abdul Wahab al-Bayati
Translated by Abdullah al-Udhari

White Jacket

The white-wool knit jacket
With a decorative pin
Which my grandpa and grandma sent me from Kovel
When I was two
And it was sent to the communal storeroom*
And I never wore it, not even once,
My God,
Grandma and Grandpa were murdered there
A whole Jewry destroyed
And I searched throughout my life
For a white-wool knit jacket
Which my grandma knit for me and decorated
With a pin
And went to the post office and sent it
In a package which my grandpa had packed lovingly
A small white hand-knitted jacket
For a little girl of two
All my life
And cannot find it.

                                        Yehudit Kafri
                                   Translated by Lami

---

*In communal Israeli settlements, kibbutzim, of the thirties, clothes for all the adults and
children were kept in and distributed from a central storeroom.

From the Diary of an Almost-Four-Year-Old

Tomorrow, the bandages
will come off. I wonder
will I see half an orange,
half an apple, half my
mother's face
with my one remaining eye?

I did not see the bullet
but felt its pain
exploding in my head.
His image did not
vanish, the soldier
with a big gun, unsteady
hands, and a look in
his eyes
I could not understand.

If I can see him so clearly
with my eyes closed,
it could be that inside our heads
we each have one spare set
of eyes
to make up for the ones we lose.

Next month, on my birthday,
I'll have a brand new glass eye,
maybe things will look round
and fat in the middle—
I've gazed through all my marbles,
they made the world look strange.

I hear a nine-month-old
has also lost an eye,
I wonder if my soldier
shot her too—a soldier
looking for little girls who
look him in the eye—
I'm old enough, almost four,
I've seen enough of life,
but she's just a baby
who didn't know any better.

Hanan Mikha'il 'Ashrawi

from The Sounds of Water's Footsteps

I am from Kashan . . .
I am a Moslem
my Mecca is a red rose
my prayer-spread the stream, my holy clay the light
my prayer-rug the field
I do ablutions to the rhythm of the rain upon the
    windowpane
In my prayer runs the moon, runs the light
the particles of my prayer have turned translucent
upon the minaret of the cypress tree
I say my prayer in the mosque of grass
and follow the sitting and rising of the wave . . .

I saw many things upon the earth:
I saw a beggar who went from door to door
singing the larks' song
I saw a poet who addressed the lily of the valley as "lady" . . .
I saw a train carrying light
I saw a train carrying politics (and going so empty)
I saw a train carrying morning-glory seeds and canary songs
and a plane, through its window
a thousand feet high, one could see the earth:
one could see the hoopoe's crest
the butterfly's beauty-spots

the passage of a fly across the alley of loneliness
the luminous wish of a sparrow descending from a pine . . .

I hear the sound of gardens breathing
the sound of the darkness raining from a leaf
the light clearing its throat behind the tree . . .
Sometimes, like a stream pebble, my soul is washed clean
   and shines
I haven't seen two pine trees hate each other
I haven't seen a poplar sell its shadow
the elm tree gives its branch to the crow at no charge
wherever there is a leaf I rejoice . . .

Sohrab Sepehri
Translated by Massud Farzan

How can I escape this busy life
when it is the cloth of every day?

✿

I sleep for six or seven hours
during which my mind never quiets down
since I return to years past
which now do not exist
and see faces
I thought had left me forever.

✿

This is a strange city.
Every time I solve one problem
ten new ones appear on the horizon.

✿

Today I realize
that my spirit has rusted
to a degree
I shall not be able
to shine it again.

✿

If the past is spread behind me
and the future is spread before me,
in this there is the comfort
of my current struggle.

Mahmud Shurayh
Translated by Aziz Shihab

But I Heard the Drops

My father had a reservoir
of tears.
They trickled down
unseen.
But I heard the drops
drip
from his voice
like drops
from a loosened tap.
For thirty years
I heard them.

Sharif S. Elmusa

from The Awakening

What happened
to the wood gatherer?
In old times he used to sing
like a bird on the shoulder of a mountain
early in the morning.
And today he doesn't speak,
he became mute
like a stone in a cave.
Who knows? Maybe he got tired.
When the river gets tired
it loves the flat lands
and the darkness of the sea.

Fuad Rifka
Translated by Aziz Shihab

The Bridge

Poetry is a river
And solitude a bridge.

Through writing
   We cross it,
Through reading

We return.

Kaissar Afif
Translated by Mansour Ajami

Give Birth to Me Again That I May Know

Give birth to me again . . . Give birth to me again that I
may know in which land I will die, in which land I
will come to life again.
Greetings to you as you light the morning fire,
greetings to you, greetings to you.
Isn't it time for me to give you some presents, to return
to you?
Is your hair still longer than our years, longer than the
trees of clouds stretching the sky to you so they can
live?
Give birth to me again so I can drink the country's milk
from you and remain a little boy in your arms, remain
a little boy
For ever. I have seen many things, mother, I have seen.
Give birth to me again so you can hold me in your
hands.
When you feel love for me, do you still sing and cry
about nothing? Mother! I have lost my hands
On the waist of a woman of a mirage. I embrace sand, I
embrace a shadow. Can I come back to you/to myself?
Your mother has a mother, the fig tree in the garden has
clouds. Don't leave me alone, a fugitive. I want your
hands

To carry my heart. I long for the bread of your voice,
    mother! I long for everything. I long for myself . . .
    I long for you.

Mahmoud Darwish
Translated by Abdullah al-Udhari

The Home Within

Once upon a tear
I tired of my fear
And my heart whispered
It's time to return
To my lonesome mommy
And my graying daddy
And the hills of olive
And shimmering dandelion.
So I packed my yearning
And began my journey
Until I arrived
At the soldiered border
That divides my world.
I handed my card
And stood in prayer
That I'd be allowed inside
Till a cold voice inquired
Didn't you know?
Time has elapsed
And your permit has expired.
Have you business there?
Sir, I don't have a business;
I have my daddy and my mommy
And many people who know me.
But that's not enough,

The guard declared.
His eyes trailed off slowly;
Then he sealed the window
And turned away.
That night I searched
For a refuge from my hurt
But could see no vein
But the path within.
From there I soared
Beyond frontier and guard
And I quickly arrived
At the old stone house
With the green door.
My father's arms
Rushed to surround me
And his thousand tears
Reached to receive me.
They cried in unison
Welcome home.

Ibtisam S. Barakat

The Beginning of the Road

He read each day like a book
and saw the world as a lantern
in the night of his fury.
He saw the horizon come to him
as a friend.
He read directions
in the faces of poetry and fire.

Adonis
Translated by Samuel Hazo

Freedom

Alone, now you are free
You pick a sky and name it
    a sky to live in
    a sky to refuse
But to know that you are free
and to remain free
you must steady yourself on a foothold of earth
so that the earth may rise
so that you may give wings to all
the children of the earth.

Saadi Youssef
Translated by Khaled Mattawa

Enough for Me

Enough for me to die on her earth
be buried in her
to melt and vanish into her soil
then sprout forth as a flower
played with by a child from my country
Enough for me to remain
in my country's embrace
to be in her close as a handful of dust
   a sprig of grass
      a flower.

Fadwa Tuqan
Translated by Salma Khadra Jayyusi
and Naomi Shihab Nye

from Stone for a Sling

. . . i played
games with childhood friends whose names i forgot
i was the best at grabbing the five stones off the ground
thanks to those five stones in one hand
i could never ever hold a sling to kill birds . . .

then i saw life-size cartoons of wars, of massacres,
of genocide . . .
of fingerprints crying out for their owners . . .
of human beings indifferent to human affliction . . .

now in my room with birds from all over the world
i play hide-and-seek in poems
hoping to shed light onto lullabies . . .
hoping not to be
the stone for a sling.

                                        Yusuf Eradam

Home

The world map
colored yellow and green
draws a straight line from Massachusetts to Egypt.

Homesick for the streets
filthy with the litter
of people, overfilled so you must
look to put your next step down;
bare feet and *galabiyas** pinch
you into a spot tighter
than a net full of fish,

drivers bound out
of their hit cars
to battle in the streets
and cause a jam as mysterious
as the building of the pyramids,

sidewalk cafes with overgrown men
heavy suited, play backgammon
and bet salaries from absent jobs,

gypsies lead their carts
with chanting voices,
tempting with the smell of crisp fried *falafel***

and cumin spiced fava beans,
sweetshops
display their *baklava* and *basboosa*†
glistening with syrup
browned like the people who make them,

women, hair and hands henna red
their eyes, *khol*-lined†† and daring.

The storms gather from the ground
dust and dirt mixed into the sand,
a whirlwind flung into my eyes,

I fly across
and land—
hands pressing into rooted earth.

Pauline Kaldas

galabiyas—kaftan-like clothes worn by Egyptians
**falafel*—delicious fried chickpea patties
†*baklava* and *basboosa*—popular Arabic sweets
††*khol*—eyeliner (makeup)

I Have No Address

I am a sparrow with a white heart and a thousand tongues.
I fly around the globe
Singing for peace, love and humanity
In every place.
I have no address.

My address is lines ornamented by dreams, beating hearts
united by smiling hope
For people who wish good for other people all the time.
I sing, smile and cry.
My tears wash away pain
In every place.

Our paths are boats of longing, turning round and round
with us—
One day to the east, another to the west, to tranquil
moorings.
And when the waves go against us and cast us away,
Then the echo of my sounds at midnight will be a dock
at the shore of tranquility,
In every place.

The day we join hands with others' hands, our universe is
A rose garden blooming in the holy night.
It contains us, with hope, love and alleluias.

And I am the sparrow on the branch.
I sleep, dream and fly happily
In every place.
I have no address.

Hamza El Din

from Memoirs in Exile

I roam from one end of time to the other,
holding in hand
my pen, my palette and my chisel.
As I look about me
I feel crippled, I've forgotten what it is
to run or jump.
I lean on my body like a cane
to cross the little space of earth
people call a homeland.
A white dot bores through a black page.
A child's tear
soaks through all the slogans.
The battle quieted down.
The old woman poked her head in
and shouted,
—Don't leave anything behind.
Ignorant people might pick your remnants up
and write our children's history with them.
Tomorrow looms in sight.
The homeland will return.
We will throw our wanderings and our suitcases
into the sea.

Joseph Abi Daher
Translated by Adnan Haydar
and Michael Beard

The Land Across the Valley
quotes from Rashid Hussein

You always told me to remember stories
about our village, and to remember
the songs that carry the legends of our land;
and to remember the faces of old women,
for in them is our history.
Isn't that so?
My father heard my words and turned away
to look across the valley to where our land is.
Teach the night to forget to bring
dreams showing me my village,
he said and then was quiet again.
His silence fell on us as the sun burned
the stones we sat on. I tried to taste
the breeze coming up from the valley.
And teach the wind to forget to carry to me
the aroma of apricots in my fields.
We looked to the other side of the valley,
at the olive trees and red poppies
scattering the hillsides.
"There is no god but Allah,"
sang a distant muezzin.
And teach the sky, too, to forget to rain.
My father closed his eyes.
Only then, may I forget my country.

Laila Halaby

rice haikus

we are women simple
sugar our morning tea
eat rice at all meals

we of simple land
kept the sugar in one sack
rice in another

lived off the brown earth
gave figs to *fidayeen**
olives and almonds

when they raided homes
they poured sugar into rice
to ruin them both

with eyelashes and
teeth we tried to sort it out
small grain from small grain

now we eat sweet rice
with our morning tea eat
meals of resistance

Suheir Hammad

*fidayeen—popular name for freedom fighters

"There Was in Our House a River"

Poem

Without paper or pen
    into your heart I reach
Listening is more poignant
    than any speech.

Fawziyya Abu Khalid
Translated by Salwa Jabsheh
and John Heath-Stubbs

Talk

You never hear it
but at breakfast the sweetest talk
is between the jam and the honey.

Gökhan Tok
Translated by Yusuf Eradam

Letters to My Mother

Good morning, sad priestess
& a kiss for your wet cheek.
It's me! Sinbad
your senseless son who
many moons ago
took off on his fantastic voyage.
Don't you remember how he packed
the green morning of home
inside his faded bag! What finesse
stuffing his clean underwear
with little bundles of dried mint leaves.

I'm alone now.
The smoke bores the cigarette.
The typewriter is bored.
The pains are birds
searching for a nest.
Yes, I've known women in America:
cement sentiments
& beauty carved of wood.

Greetings to our large house
to my bed & books
to the children of our block
to walls we decorated with chaotic writing

to lazy cats sleeping on windowsills
covered with lilacs.

Twelve years now, Mother
since I left Tangier.
November is here
He brings his presents pressingly:
tears & moans at my window pane
& November is here.
Where is Tangier?
Its saffron suns & listless seas?
Where is Father?
Where are his eyes
& the silk of their look?
Where is the open yard
of our large house?
Carnations chuckled
in the shade of its corners.
Where is my childhood?
I dragged cats by their tails
across the open yard.

I'm alone now.
My pains are birds searching for a nest.

                              Ben Bennani

I Do Not Blame You

Your wings are small for this storm—
I do not blame you.
You're good, and frightened, and
I am the hurricane. I used to be a wing
struggling in the storm
but then I became the storm,
lacking light, shade, or a wise language.
And now I confess
to be a lost planet circling a lost world
and I do not blame you:
What has tender mint to do with the storm?

Samih al-Qasim
Translated by Sharif S. Elmusa
and Naomi Shihab Nye

The River

Once
there was in our house a river
magnanimous
delicate steps
My father made his rosary from its minnows
and the carpet we spread was made from its mist
Once
a thief came to our house
He came from beyond the villages
and axes were landed on his neck
and split him in halves
Since then
My father's heart dried up and he died
My sisters ended up in poverty and widowhood
But my mother insisted
on digging the earth
scratching with her fingers
believing water will appear

Hashim Shafiq
Translated by Khaled Mattawa

A Song

When we remember things
One string rings out.
Woman alone
Plays on all the strings
With one stroke
Because she is the entire homeland.

Muhammad al-As'ad
Translated by May Jayyusi
and Jack Collom

All of Them

Everybody said it was useless
Everybody said, "you're trying to lean on sun dust"
   that the beloved before whose tree I stand
      can't be reached

Everybody said, "you're crazy to throw yourself
   headlong into a volcano and sing"
Everybody said that salty mountains
   won't yield even one glass of wine
Everybody said, "You can't dance on one foot"
Everybody said there won't be any lights at the party
That's what they all said
but everybody came to the party anyway

Qasim Haddad
Translated by Sharif S. Elmusa
and Charles Doria

Electrons

Atoms within your body
spin.
What seems solid—
knees, nose, hair—
moves swiftly. Particles
orbit each other. Dart like meteors
through vast spaces.

Air about you
made of same.
You take from it
and you give.
Drawing in atoms and molecules
to form
your ever changing image.

Your lips move.
Your tongue speaks your name.
You take it on faith your words will make sense.
Meaning flows out effortlessly.

Electrons
skip like rocks on water
between your solid body
and your electromagnetic thoughts.

You look through a window.
Listen to voices from within and without.
Dazzled by what you perceive,
you wonder about causes and effects.

When a wave of love takes you by surprise,
your eyes well up with tears.

Assef al-Jundi

from Thread by Thread

Thread by thread
knot by knot
like colonies of ants
we weave a bridge

Thread by thread
piece by piece
knitting embroidering
sewing decorating
thread by thread
we weave
the map of conciliation.

Rachel's is white
Yemima's purple
Amal's is green
Salima's rose-colored
thread by thread
we stitch together
torn hearts
bind the map of conciliation.

I pray for the life of Ami and Nitsi
you pray for Ilan, Shoshi and Itsik
and she prays

for Jehan, Asheraf and Fahed
with the same tear.
Word and another word
prayer and another prayer
and our heart is one
we embroider in hope
with the sisterhood of workers
a map of love
to tear down the borders . . .

Bracha Serri
Translated by Shlomit Yaacobi
and Nava Mizrahhi

The Deserted Well

I knew Ibrahim
my dear neighbor
from way back. I knew
him overflowing with water
like a well people passed by
without stopping to drink
or even, even to drop
a stone.

When the enemy aimed
their cannon of death
and the soldiers rushed
under a hail of death
and shelling, *retreat! retreat!*
it was shouted, *in the shelter*
back there, you shall
be safe from death
and shelling.
But Ibrahim
kept marching on
his tiny breast filling
the horizon, he marched forward
retreat! retreat!
in the shelter back there
you shall be safe

from death
and shelling.
But Ibrahim
as though he didn't hear
kept on marching.
They said it was madness.
Maybe it was madness.
But I had known
my dear neighbor Ibrahim
from way back. From childhood I knew him
overflowing with water
like a well people passed by
without stopping to drink
or even, even to drop
a stone

Yusuf al-Khal
Translated by Sargon Boulus

A Day in the Life of Nablus

We fall, not on our knees, but on our hearts
—Vassar Miller

-1-

Summer. The figs are bruise pink,
tomatoes luscious enough
to stop a hurried man.
Ignore the flies.
At 9 a.m. peasants savor *shish-kebab*
in puny, vaulted eateries.
Ah, the roasting coffee's aroma,
the folklore of each of the senses

This is a place for commerce.
Everything here is for sale:
children's toys, kitchen utensils,
bananas, peanuts, pinenuts, posters,
cassettes, straw mats, sponge mats, watches,
Elvis' T-shirts, turkey breasts, shoes.

The vendor in dishevelled clothes
arranges a feast of pears,
lifts one with pride
as he might his own child.
He bellows into the air:
Go to sleep with a sweet mouth.
He sees the soldiers.
He does not brood over power or history.

-2-

No curfew
during our five-week stay.

-3-

Walking on University Boulevard,
I spot soldiers manning a checkpoint:
the school has been ordered shut.
And, as if in the recurring dream,
I frisk myself for my passport
but find my pockets empty.
I go past the black machine guns
thinking how as a boy
I caught black wasps
and removed their stingers.

A few yards away from the checkpoint
I read a sign:
Office of Reconciliation.
Inside, a Samaritan rabbi
clad in brown caftan and red turban
is ensconced on a couch, waiting,
resigned to waiting.

-4-

On an immaculate wall
of a friend's living room
hangs a picture in a gilded frame:
a woman squatting amidst the rubble
of her house demolished by the army,
cheek cupped in hand,
peering into a white, empty bucket.

-5-

In cafes men congregate in the afternoons,
slowly sip their tea
(as if time were their own),
shuffle cards, spur the backgammon dice
(as if chance were their own).
They listen to songs
of unrequited love, promises unkept, partings.
When the sun sinks behind the hills
they salute the fading day, irreconciled,
leaving the folded market
to the screech of armored cars.

-6-

The sky flowers tonight.
The Stars are bright and real
as children's eyes
as the faces of women loved
after years of waiting.

A meteor dives like a deft acrobat.
A satellite sails west to east, unperturbed.
Is it Russian or American?
A scientist or a spy?
Or a station where voices
of distant lovers dovetail?
In gowns of soft lights
the town performs the ritual of sleep.
Will the vendor,
will the woman who lost her house
sleep with a sweet mouth?
The settlement, fortress on the mountain peak,
and the jail on the hilltop
flood their dreams with yellow lights.

I want the kind breeze
the power of pears
the sound of the flute,
melodious and sad
like the hills of this land,
to grant us all,
vendors and soldiers,
grant us ample love
that we may turn this troubled page
that we may sleep with a sweet mouth.

Sharif S. Elmusa

Quintrain

Once . . . I heard a bird,
an absorbed, ecstatic bird,
eloquently telling
its child:
"Fly away,
soar high:
a few bread crumbs
will suffice you,
but the sky
you need . . .
the whole sky."

Sa'id 'Aql
Translated by Mansour Ajami

Notes on the Contributors

ADONIS (b. 1930, Syria) is one of the most widely loved poets, critics, translators, philosophers, and presenters of poetry in the Arab world. He works in literary journalism in Lebanon and has published many books, including *The Pages of Day and Night*.

GÜLTEN AKIN (b. 1933) is one of Turkey's most distinguished and quoted women poets, for whom "poetry is synonymous with social responsibility." She has worked as a lawyer in Anatolia and currently lives in Ankara.

LAYLA 'ALLUSH (b. 1948, Palestine) has written extensively about life under occupation. Her first book was called *Spices on the Open Wound*.

SA'ID 'AQL (b. 1912, Lebanon) is well-known for influencing Arabic poetry toward Symbolism. One of his books is called *More Beautiful Than You, No!*

HANAN MIKHA'IL 'ASHRAWI (b. 1946, Palestine) became known worldwide for her efforts in Palestinian-Israeli negotiations toward peace. Her autobiography is called *This Side of Peace* (Simon & Schuster). She received a doctorate in Medieval English Literature and headed the English Department at Bir Zeit University. She lives in Ramallah with her husband, a musician.

MUHAMMAD AL-AS'AD (b. 1944, Palestine) lived first in a village near Haifa, but his family moved to Iraq after becoming refugees in 1948. He has worked as a journalist in Kuwait, has published an autobiography, poetry, and criticism, and currently lives in Cyprus.

IBTISAM S. BARAKAT (b. 1963) grew up in the occupied territories of Palestine and attended Bir Zeit University where she studied English Literature. She came to the United States to study journalism and human development, has written for children and been a publications editor, and currently lives in Missouri.

ABDUL WAHAB AL-BAYATI (b. 1926, Iraq) studied at Baghdad Teachers College and worked as a teacher, then a journalist. He has lived in Lebanon, Syria, Egypt, Austria, and Moscow, and is considered one of the most important representatives of the "socialist realist school" in modern Arabic poetry.

ZEYNEP BELER (b. 1985, Ankara) started painting when she was a baby. She lives in Turkey, where she likes reading and writing poems and stories, and has exhibitions of her paintings. She was twelve when she wrote the poem in this book.

BEN BENNANI (b. 1946, Lebanon) was educated in classical Arabic literature in Tripoli. He has taught writing, translation, and literature in the United States and Bahrain. His poems and translations have been published widely; one book of poems is called *Camel's Bite*.

EDIP CANSEVER (1928–1986) grew up in Istanbul. He began publishing in 1944 and received numerous awards for his work.

SHLOMIT COHEN-ASSIF is a native Israeli who lives and writes in Holon. A prolific author of children's books, poems, and fairy tales, she reads her work widely and received the 1996 ACUM prize for Life Contribution to the Arts.

JOSEPH ABI DAHER (b. 1947, Lebanon) entered the world of journalism at an early age. He has founded literary magazines, published books of poetry, written hundreds of TV and radio shows, and songs and plays for children. He is also a painter. UNICEF awarded him a prize for his children's songs in 1986.

MAHMOUD DARWISH (b. 1942, Palestine) is one of the most honored voices worldwide for the Palestinian people. He grew up in Birwa and Haifa and has lived in Egypt, Lebanon, and Paris.

HAMZA EL DIN (b. 1929, Wadi-Halfa, near the Egypt-Sudan border) has been called "the living ambassador of Nubian music." He began playing the *oud* and vocalizing during college. The village he lived in as a child was flooded by the construction of the Aswan Dam. "At that time in Egypt, between every coffee shop and the next coffee shop, there was a coffee shop, and each coffee shop had a radio. When you walked down the street you continuously heard music." He travels widely to perform.

MOSHE DOR was born in Tel Aviv and has published numerous volumes of poetry and literary essays. He worked as a journalist and writer-in-residence for many years and has received many honors, including the Prime Minister's Prize and the Bialik Prize, Israel's top literary award.

SHARIF S. ELMUSA (b. 1947, Palestine) was the fifth in a family of twelve children made refugees within a year of his birth. His father grew figs, grapes, and oranges outside Jaffa till the family moved to the Nuweimeh refugee camp in Jericho. Elmusa attended Cairo University and received his Ph.D. from M.I.T. An expert on agrarian development and water issues, he teaches both in the Middle East and Washington, D.C.

YUSUF ERADAM (b. 1954, Turkey) is a prolific poet, translator, short-story writer, songwriter, and editor currently teaching American Literature at Ankara University.

SALAH FA'IQ (b. 1945, Iraq) left school at the age of fifteen and has worked as a journalist and literary editor, publishing collections of prose poetry.

QASIM HADDAD (b. 1948, Bahrain) left secondary school before graduation and later became Director of Culture and Art at the Ministry of Information. He has also headed the Union of Bahraini Writers and has been published widely.

LAILA HALABY was born in Lebanon, the daughter of a Jordanian father and American mother. She lives in Los Angeles and is fluent in Spanish, Arabic, Italian, and French. She has master's degrees in Arabic Literature and counseling and received a Fulbright scholarship to Jordan.

SUHEIR HAMMAD (b. 1973, Jordan) is the daughter of Palestinian refugee parents. Her family lived in Beirut during part of the Civil War, then immigrated to Brooklyn, New York. She is devoted to "giving voice to those who have been silenced for so long." Her books are *Drops of This Story* and *Born Palestinian, Born Black*.

NATHALIE HANDAL was born in 1969 into a family from Bethlehem, Palestine. She grew up in the Caribbean and Europe, but returns to the Middle East often. She received her M.A. in Literature in Boston and is now a researcher/scholar writing and lecturing on Arab and Arab-American women writers. Her most recent book of poetry is *The Neverfield*. She lives in New York and London.

NAZIM HIKMET (1902–1963) is considered the poet laureate of Turkey. He was a political prisoner in Turkey for nineteen years and spent the last thirteen years of his life in exile. His work was banned in Turkey for decades. Many of his film scripts, plays, essays, and novels were published after his death. Now he is revered and quoted worldwide by people supporting human rights and peace.

MOHAMMED AFIF HUSSAINI is a Syrian poet living in Sweden.

TAHAR BEN JELLOUN is a novelist and poet of Morocco, writing in French.

ASSEF AL-JUNDI (b. 1952, Damascus) grew up in Syria and came to the United States to study electrical engineering in Texas. He returned to Syria to work in the oil fields and now lives in San Antonio where he works for a telecommunications company.

SHAFEE'E KADKANI of Iran, a university professor, wrote works which were widely known both before and after the revolution.

YEHUDIT KAFRI (b. 1935, Kibbutz Ein Ha Horesh) works in editing, translating, and writing in Israel and has received awards for her poetry, children's books, memoirs, and biographies.

PAULINE KALDAS (b. Egypt) came to the United States in 1969. After several months, she was able to decipher the English language and went on to repeat the fourth grade successfully. She often missed her grandmother, her dog Rita, and the guava tree in her Egyptian backyard. She has returned to Egypt more than once and has taught in Cairo and New York.

YUSUF AL-KHAL (1917–1987, Lebanon) was the son of a Protestant minister. He studied philosophy and worked in the United States, Libya, and Switzerland. He founded the Shi'r quarterly and publishing house which promoted experimental poetry and translated American poets into Arabic. He also did new translations of the New and Old Testaments.

FAWZIYYA ABU KHALID (b. 1955, Saudia Arabia) grew up in Riyadh, studied sociology in the United States, and has taught at the Girls' College of King Saud University. Her first book of poems was published when she was eighteen.

DEEMA SHEHABI KHORSHEED is a Palestinian who grew up in Kuwait. After graduating from Boston University with a master's degree in journalism, she moved to northern California, where she now resides.

SAMI MAHDI (b. 1940, Iraq) studied economics in Baghdad and became editor-in-chief of one of Iraq's leading newspapers, *Al-Jumhuriya*. He has published numerous collections of poetry, including *The Questions*.

LISA SUHAIR MAJAJ was born to a Palestinian father and an American mother and grew up in Jordan. She studied in Lebanon before moving to the United States and completing a doctorate on Arab-American Literature. She currently lives in Cyprus.

MAY MANSOOR MUNN (b. 1934, Jerusalem) loved to read as a child. Her parents were Palestinian Quakers. She began writing poetry during the violent times of 1948, when thousands of Palestinians lost homes and property to the new state of Israel. At fifteen she traveled via ocean liner to the United States to attend college, leaving four younger sisters behind. Later she returned home to work as a teacher and disc jockey. She now lives in Texas.

SAMIH AL-QASIM (b.1939, Jordan) is a Palestinian living in Nazareth. He has said, "The only way I can assert my identity is by writing poetry." He has worked as a journalist, run a press and folk arts center, read his poems widely, and been imprisoned many times for his political activities. "I feel there is no spiritual difference between Baghdad or Tunis or Jerusalem. I feel that all those countries belong to me. They are my homeland."

ABDUL-RAHEEM SALEH AL-RAHEEM (b. 1950, Iraq) received an M.A. in counseling and has been publishing his poems in Iraqi newspapers and magazines since the Seventies. He is married and has six children. "The Train of the Stars" is the title poem of his book.

FUAD RIFKA (b. 1930, Lebanon) has a Ph.D. in philosophy and lives and teaches in Beirut. He has published many collections of poems.

GLADYS ALAM SAROYAN writes: "'Unveiled' is about becoming visible. I was born invisible in Beirut, Lebanon. I was not a male, or even a girl of unusual beauty. My hair is black, my eyes are brown . . . I am the middle child of a family of five . . . (Now) I am unveiling. And to my surprise, under my veil, smiles a real face." This is her first publication in a book.

SOHRAB SEPEHRI (b. 1928, Iran) is considered to be one of the most gifted poets writing in Persian. He has published many books and is also a painter.

BRACHA SERRI was born and grew up in Yemen until her family moved to Israel. She writes: "I'm trying to make peace with my pieces. I want my mother's Yemenite culture to be at peace with my father's Jewishness. I want my childhood-spoken language, Arabic, to come together with my university education in linguistics. . . . I feel I have written my poems for women who do not have a voice, who can't speak up for themselves."

ABU-L-QASIM AL-SHABBI (1909-1934) is considered Tunisia's most beloved poet of the twentieth century, despite his very short life. He was born in Tawzur in the palm-grove district, but his family moved constantly from one town to another during his childhood. He was first published at the age of eighteen. Shortly after his marriage, he died of cardiac disease, but his poetry became well known all over the Arab world.

HASHIM SHAFIQ was born and grew up in Iraq. He currently lives and writes poetry in Arabic in London.

MOHAMMED SHEHADEH is a Palestinian poet and doctor living in Jerusalem.

REZA SHIRAZI is Iranian, grew up in India where he wrote his first poem about the Taj Mahal at the age of eight, and currently lives in Texas.

MAHMUD M. SHURAYH (b. 1952, Lebanon) studied English and philosophy at the American University of Beirut. He has worked as a translator, teacher, writer on cultural affairs, and editor of modern Arabic poetry, and currently lives in France.

RONNY SOMECK (b. 1951, Baghdad) immigrated to Israel as a child. He has published many collections of poems and translations and received the Prime Minister's Prize in 1989.

GÜKHAN TOK (b. 1972, Ankara) graduated from the sociology department of the Middle East Technical University and works at The Turkish Foundation of Science and Research.

NADIA TUÉNI lived in Lebanon and died in 1983. She wrote many books of poems, including *Lebanon: Twenty Poems for One Love,* and was married to the former Ambassador of Lebanon to the United Nations.

KEMALETTIN TUĞCU (1902–1996) is one of the legends of Turkish popular writing. He was unable to walk and attended no schools. He wrote stories, poems, and novels, many about the grief of poor children, and eventually published more than five hundred books. He considered himself "the richest man on earth" and wrote actively till his death, though he could barely hear or see in his last years.

FADWA TUQAN (b. 1917, Palestine) grew up in the town of Nablus, where she still lives. Her brother gave her private lessons at home in lieu of formal secondary school. She learned English and literature at Oxford, England. Her works became increasingly political as the Palestinian/Israeli conflict intensified. With her poems translated into numerous languages, she is considered one of the treasures of the Arabic literary world.

SADDI YOUSSEF is one of the leading Iraqi poets, whose work is well known all over the Arab world. He lives in Paris.

LORENE ZAROU-ZOUZOUNIS (b. 1958, Palestine) used to help her grandmother sweep her patio, and pick wild herbs and greens in the fields near their home. She writes, "The smell of narcissus brings me home more than anything, as this flower filled the valleys and hills." She now lives in California.

Acknowledgments

I am grateful to all who assisted this project, especially: Nathalie Handal, Sharif S. Elmusa, and Khaled Mattawa.

The landmark labors of Dr. Salma Khadra Jayyusi of PROTA (Project of Translation from Arabic) have been an immense gift to our cultural heritage and we will never stop thanking her. Her anthologies are classics in the field.

My gratitude also to: Barbara Nimri Aziz; Elie Chalala of *Al Jadid* magazine; the music of Hamza El Din, Ali Jihad Racy, and Simon Shaheen; to Samuel Hazo of the International Poetry Forum in Pittsburgh for everything, always. Thanks to RAWI, the Radius of Arab-American Writers; Aziz Shihab; Miriam Allwardt Shihab; and Virginia Duncan, my hero.

And large hugs to the staff at Simon & Schuster Children's Publishing, especially Julia Richardson—it was a pleasure to work together on this paperback edition.

Naomi Shihab Nye

Index to Poets

Index to Poems